Learn Spanish Grammar NOW!

Antonio Del Torro

Minute Help Press

www.minutehelp.com

Table of Contents

Introduction

Spanish is one of the largest, most widely spoken languages in the world. If you live in the US, chances are you know someone who speaks it. Spanish, next to Mandarin Chinese, is probably one of the most economically advantageous languages to learn. Being able to communicate in Spanish can add a few extra thousand dollars to your yearly paycheck, as well as endear you to the Spanish speaking community where you live. But don't just do it for the money; the Spanish language is responsible for some of the most beautiful music, films, and literature in the world. Having access to this extraordinarily rich culture is reason enough to start learning Spanish.

This guide provides a quick survey of Spanish grammar, providing easy-to-understand information on nouns, verbs, adjectives, and all the other grammatical nuances that you need to know to go out there and start speaking. It's a brief guide, but don't worry...Spanish is not that complicated!

If you're just starting out or have taken classes previously and need a refresher, this guide will help you. Get ready to learn Spanish grammar NOW!

Nouns

Nouns name people, places, things, and ideas. Unlike English, Spanish divides its nouns into different genders (masculine and feminine) and is accompanied by either a definite or indefinite article. First, examine the articles and observe how they agree with their nouns.

Definite articles – "the"

	SINGULAR	PLURAL
MASCULINE	el	los
FEMININE	la	las

Indefinite articles – "a, an; some"

	SINGULAR	PLURAL
MASCULINE	un	unos
FEMININE	una	unas

While it may seem cumbersome to learn the gender of each noun, there are some simple guidelines to follow. Remember that the gender of a noun is based on the structure of the word itself, not what the word means, not who uses it, nor who owns it.

Nouns that refer to people reflect the gender of the person named.

Masculine	Feminine
el padre, el hombre, un maestro, un muchacho	la madre, la mujer, una maestra, una muchacha

As a general rule, nouns that end in –o are masculine while nouns that end in –a are feminine.

Masculine	Feminine
el libro, el cuaderno,	la mochila, la puerta,

It is best to learn the gender of the article when you learn a new vocabulary word rather than applying the following rules that appear to be exceptions to the aforementioned simplistic distinction. However, knowing how those rules operate is useful for long-term retention. You will also see that as you continue to learn new vocabulary and you can make the "exceptions" fit into these smaller rules, it will become apparent that the vast majority of vocabulary behaves in an entirely predictable fashion. Then, when the out-and-out exceptions do occur, you'll be able to remember them that much better.

- Nouns that end in *-ción, -sión, -dad,* and *-tud* are all feminine. You'll also note that the nouns that fall into this category are what are known as cognates – words between two languages that are nearly or exactly identical to each other. This helps to relieve the brunt memorization of much vocabulary, and in time you'll discover that you may actually be able to create the correct Spanish word without having explicitly learned it previously.

la lección (lesson)	*la tensión* (tension)	*la ciudad* (city)	*la actitud* (attitude)
la selección (selection)	*la admisión* (admission)	*la generosidad* (generosity)	*la multitud* (multitude)
la loción (lotion)	*la sesión* (session)	*la posibilidad* (possibility)	*la plentitud* (plentitude)
la posición (position)	*la ilusión* (illusion)	*la realidad* (reality)	*la latitud* (latitude)

- Many nouns that end in *-ma, -pa,* and *-ta* are typically masculine, however this is not an absolute rule.

el clima (climate)	*el programa* (program)	*el tema* (theme)	*el planeta* (planet)
el sistema (system)		*el mapa* (map)	*el cometa* (comet)
	el drama (drama)		

- There are a few nouns that completely defy categorization into neat rules. The best approach is to simply memorize them as they are: *el día (day),* **la mano** *(hand),* **la foto** *(photo),* and **la moto** *(abbreviated form of motorcycle).*

As much as you need to concern yourself with the gender of a noun, you'll also need to consider the number – whether the noun is singular or plural. Always maintain agreement between nouns and their articles. When you need to make a noun plural, follow these simple rules.

- If a noun ends in a vowel, simply add an -s to the end of the noun:
  el padre, los padres; una muchacha, unas muchachas
- If a noun ends in a consonant, add -es to the end of the noun
  la lección, las lecciones; un salon, unos salones
- If a noun ends in a -z, change the -z to -c, and then add -es.
  el lápiz, los lapices; una luz, unas luces

There is one final detail regarding collective nouns that bears mentioning. These are nouns which refer to many people or things at once, but remain singular. The key will be to always use a singular verb in order to maintain subject-verb agreement. Some of these collective nouns will be entirely intuitive to use; others you should merely disregard the actual meaning of the noun and rely on the fact that it is indeed a singular noun, and should therefore take a singular verb. In the following examples, the collective nouns are underlined.

<u>La familia</u> vive en un apartamento en la ciudad.

<u>The family</u> lives in an apartment in the city.

<u>La clase</u> es en la cafetería hoy en vez del salón.

<u>The class</u> is in the cafeteria today instead of the classroom.

<u>La gente</u> escucha atentamente al político durante el debate.

<u>The people</u> listen attentively to the politician during the debate.

<u>La policía</u> detuvo a <u>la muchedumbre</u> después del debate.

<u>The police</u> detained <u>the crowd</u> after the debate.

Pronouns

In Spanish as well as English there are different kinds of pronouns that allow us to replace nouns in order to avoid redundancy. To begin with, you will first encounter subject and object pronouns. In grammatical terms, the nouns to which the pronouns refer are known as the antecedents. In Spanish, you must always maintain agreement between any antecedent and pronoun pair – think back to the previous discussion regarding gender and number. This constant agreement aids tremendously in creating the grand and highly regulated scheme that is Spanish grammar.

Subject pronouns: The most necessary pronouns for communication in Spanish are subject pronouns. These, along with the actual subjects themselves, hold the capacity to determine verb forms and therefore hold an integral role in commanding basic sentence structure. Subjects explain who or what performs the action of the verb. Your verb form will be dictated by the subject, whether noun or pronoun. Compare what you already know about the English language; it carries directly over into Spanish.

English Subject Pronouns			Spanish Subject Pronouns		
	SINGULAR	PLURAL		SINGULAR	PLURAL
FIRST PERSON	I	we	FIRST PERSON	yo	nosotros, nosotras
SECOND PERSON	you	all of you (y'all)	SECOND PERSON	tú	
THIRD PERSON	he she (it)	they	THIRD PERSON	él ella usted	ellos ellas ustedes

At this point, you'll need to take into account a few very important distinctions that occur within the Spanish language.

- As a subject pronoun, the word "it" does not exist in Spanish. You'll notice that **usted** appears in the corresponding position on the chart. **Usted** is one of three ways to express "you" in Spanish. Rarely will you see the word in its entirety in print. **Ud.** and its plural **Uds.** are far more common, yet you still pronounce them as whole words. When used as abbreviations, they are always capitalized.

- Familiar vs. Formal address: When addressing a person with the pronoun "you," it is necessary to take into account the level of formality required in the given situation. **Tú** is utilized with people who you consider your friends, people who are of your same social status and age (or younger), people who you are very well-acquainted with – think of your best friend, your family members, your co-workers. **Usted**, on the other hand, is reserved to be used with people to whom you have been introduced for the first time, people who are of a high-ranking social status or in a role of authority over you, and people for whom you believe are entitled to an extra special measure of respect – think of your boss' wife, a police officer, your elderly grandmother. Each of the Latin American cultures has a slightly different read on who merits the familiar or formal address. When in doubt, the best solution is to remain formal, use **usted,** and take your clue from the other person. When you receive the go-ahead, proceed in a familiar fashion and use **tú**.

- Singular vs. Plural: In English, we refer to one person to whom we are speaking as simply "you." We also naturally transition to a colloquial plural version – commonly "you" or even "you guys"; "y'all" in the

South; perhaps even "youse guys" in the Bronx. In Spanish, this is not as much of a regional difference as an actual grammatical one. When addressing more than one person as a group, you should use **Uds.** (In Spain, this is a more complex issue. Just as we saw a familiar and a formal singular form of you (*tú* and **Ud.**), Spain holds with a distinction in the plural forms as well – *vosotros*. As this article focuses solely on Latin American Spanish, it will suffice to say that the pronoun **Uds.** functions in both the familiar and formal capacity.

- Masculine vs. Feminine: You will notice that the distinction in gender carries over into the realm of pronouns as well. It is easy to see that *él* is "he" and that *ella* is "she." But, you'll want to consider how to best assign gender to the groups of "we" and "they." The rule applies equally to both the usage of *nosotros* and *ellos*: when referring to a group of females, use the feminine form and to a group of males, the masculine form. But what to do with a group of mixed genders? Always use the masculine form.

Indefinite pronouns: As their name would indicate, indefinite pronouns refer to someone or something that is not specifically named. Frequently these pronouns function as subjects of sentences and they should take the third person, singular form that corresponds with *él or ella*. Study the following set of indefinite pronouns.

alguien (someone)   *nadie* (no one)   *algo* (something)   *nada* (nothing)

Alguien nos llama por teléfono.	*Someone is calling us on the telephone.*
Nadie lo contesta.	*No one is answering it.*
Algo está en el árbol...¿Qué es?	*Something is in the tree...What is it?*
Nada puede ser tan feo.	*Nothing can be so ugly.*

Direct object pronouns: Another set of important pronouns to utilize are direct object pronouns. These replace the direct object in order to avoid redundancy. Consider the following set of English sentences:

I can't find my new jacket. I looked for my new jacket in the closet. I looked for my new jacket in the living room. Do you know where my new jacket is? Oh, yes. I put my new jacket in my bedroom.

Obviously, the usage of the phrase "my new jacket" is repetitive and the passage can be reworked to be much more concise with the usage of a direct object pronoun.

I can't find my new jacket. I looked for it in the closet and in the living room. Do you know where it is? Oh, yes. I put it in my bedroom.

Just as you've seen before, maintaining agreement is essential. Once again, any direct object pronoun must agree with its antecedent. Review the following set of English and Spanish direct object pronouns (DOP).

English Direct Object Pronouns			Spanish Direct Object Pronouns		
	SINGULAR	PLURAL		SINGULAR	PLURAL
FIRST PERSON	me	us	FIRST PERSON	me	Nos
SECOND PERSON	you	all of you (y'all)	SECOND PERSON	te	
THIRD PERSON	him her it you (formal)	them you (plural)	THIRD PERSON	lo la	los las

It is important to recognize that DOP placement in Spanish differs from English. Rather than appearing after the verb in English, notice that DOPs commonly appear *before* the verb in Spanish. Follow these rules of placement:

- Always place the DOP before a conjugated verb. Notice that this applies to compound verbs as well.

La busqué en el armario. La había puesto en mi dormitorio. I looked for *it* in the closet. I had put *it* in my bedroom.

- The DOP may be attached to the end of an infinitive or a gerund. (Note that there are two means of expression as these sentences also contain a conjugated verb.)

Necesito encontrarla. Estoy buscándola ahora mismo. I need to find *it*. I am looking for *it* right now.

La necesito encontrar. La estoy buscando ahora mismo.

Indirect object pronouns: Closely related to direct object pronouns are indirect object pronouns, and these operate in the same fashion. Invariably, indirect objects refer to people whereas direct objects may refer to either people or things. Easily stated, the indirect object answers the question *To whom?* or *For whom?* Consider the following set of indirect object pronouns (IOP):

English Indirect Object Pronouns			Spanish Indirect Object Pronouns		
	SINGULAR	PLURAL		SINGULAR	PLURAL
FIRST PERSON	to / for me	to / for us	FIRST PERSON	me	nos
SECOND PERSON	to / for you	to / for all of you (y'all)	SECOND PERSON	te	
THIRD PERSON	to / for him to / for her to / for you (form.)	to / for them to / for you (plural)	THIRD PERSON	le	les

While DOPs replace their DOs, IOPs are designed to **reinforce** their IOs, and although it seems redundant, you will typically use both the antecedent and the pronoun in the same sentence.

> **Ella *me* regaló un libro *a mí*.**　　　　*She gave a book to me.*
>
> **Elena *nos* compró la cena *a nosotros*.**　　*Elena bought dinner for us.*

Just as with DOPs, IOPs follow the same rules of placement, generally appearing before conjugated verbs. However, the question remains how to manage a situation in which you would like to use both pronouns together. The correct order of pronouns will always be ***indirect, direct (ID)***.

> **Ella *me* regaló un libro *a mí*. Ella *me* lo regaló *a mí*.**　　*She gave a book to me. She gave it to me.*
>
> 　　　　　　　　　　　　　　　　　　*Elena bought dinner for us. Elena bought*

*Elena **nos** compró la cena **a nosotros**.*   *it **for us**.*

*Ella **nos la** compró a nosotros.*

One final note: You'll notice an awkward alliteration occurs when you combine third person object pronouns together. When this occurs, simply change the IOP (*le / les*) to *se*:

*Ella **le** dio un regalo **a mi madre**.*   Incorrect: *Ella **le lo** dio **a mi madre**.*

                                                                      Correct: *Ella **se lo** dio **a mi madre**.*

Possessive pronouns: Possessive pronouns do precisely what their name indicates – they indicate possession without specifically naming the noun that is owned. Consider the following charts which compare English and Spanish. Note that because the possessive pronoun ends in **–o**, it generates four forms to be able to maintain agreement between masculine or feminine antecedents.

English Possessive Pronouns			Spanish Possessive Pronouns				
FIRST PERSON	mine	ours	FIRST PERSON	el mio los mios la mia las mias		el nuestro los nuestros la nuestra las nuestras	
SECOND PERSON	yours		SECOND PERSON	el tuyo los tuyos la tuya las tuyas			
THIRD PERSON	his hers your (formal)	theirs yours (plural)	THIRD PERSON	el suyo los suyos la suya las suyas		el suyo los suyos la suya las suyas	

Now, study the following examples:

¿Es <u>mi</u> libro? Sí, es <u>tuyo</u>.		*Is it my book? Yes, it is yours.*
¿Son <u>tus</u> zapatos? Sí, son <u>míos</u>.		*Are they your shoes? Yes, they are mine.*
¿Dónde está <u>su</u> chaqueta? <u>La suya</u> está en el ropero.		*Where is her (his) jacket? Hers (His) is in the closet.*
¿Son <u>nuestras</u> maletas? No. <u>Las nuestras</u> son negras.		*Are they our suitcases? No. Ours are black.*
¿Han visto <u>sus</u> fotos del viaje? Sí, las suyas son fantásticas.		*Have you seen their pictures of the trip? Yes, theirs are fantastic.*

Demonstrative pronouns: Demonstrative pronouns indicate which one of an item you are referring to. You'll notice that these are essentially the same words that are used as demonstrative adjectives. For an easy test to tell the difference between the two, consider that a pronoun replaces a noun and therefore will appear by itself; on the other hand, a demonstrative adjective modifies a noun and will appear immediately before it.

this one/ these ones here – indicating an item that is close to the speaker			that one / those ones there – indicating an item that is at a short distance from the speaker			that one / those ones over there – indicating an item that is at a significant distance from the speaker		
	SINGULAR	PLURAL		SINGULAR	PLURAL		SINGULAR	PLURAL
MASCULINE	este	estos	MASCULINE	ese	esos	MASCULINE	aquel	aquellos
FEMININE	esta	estas	FEMININE	esa	esas	FEMININE	aquella	aquellas

As you now examine some examples in context, you'll see that it is exceedingly important to clearly name the antecedent so as to avoid any confusion.

¿Prefieres estos zapatos aquí o <u>aquellos</u> allá?	*Do you prefer <u>these</u> shoes <u>here</u> or <u>those over</u>*

*Me gustan **esos** que tiene Mamá.*

there?

*I like **those** that Mom has.*

*¿Cuáles de las galletas quieres? **¿Esas** con chocolate o **aquellas** con canela?*

*Which of the cookies do you want? **These** chocolate **ones** (**there**) or **those** cinnamon **ones** (**over there**)?*

*No quiero ningunas de **esas**. Quiero **estas** de menta.*

*I don't want any of **these**. I want **these** mint **ones** (**that are right here**).*

Relative pronouns: Relative pronouns perform a slightly different task than other pronouns in that they serve to connect a clause (a group of words that contains both a subject and a verb) to its antecedent. This clause provides more information about the noun much like an adjective does but is larger than a single word. The most common relative pronouns are **que** *(that)* and **quien** *(who)*. As in English, you may apply **que** to either people or things, but you may only apply **quien** to people. Observe the following examples – the entire relative clause is underlined:

*Quiero comprar el coche **que tiene espacio para seis pasajeros**.*

*I want to buy the car **that has room for six passengers**.*

*Hablo con una mujer **que está visitando nuestro país**.*

*I'm speaking with a woman **that is visiting our country**.*

*Vivo con mi amiga **quien es de El Salvador**.*

*I'm living with my friend **who is from El Salvador**.*

*Conocemos a las personas **quienes eran estudiantes de intercambio**.*

*We met the people **who were exchange students**.*

Note: Be aware that **quien** will need to be made plural (**quienes**) whenever its antecedent is plural.

Adjectives

Adjectives are the words that add description to our nouns. As you have seen with articles and pronouns, maintaining agreement is essential – *always think: masculine, feminine; singular, plural*. When changing adjectives from singular to plural, you will follow the same rules as you did previously with nouns. Additionally, adjust for masculine or feminine adjectives by alternating between *–o* and *–a* as needed.

Aside from this perpetual characteristic, it is the fact that most adjectives are placed *after* the nouns they modify instead of *before* them that gives Spanish the reputation of being a language that is "backward." Consider the following adjective phrases that include nouns with their respective articles and adjectives.

FEMININE	the black purse	the red blouses

		negros
FEMININE	la bolsa negra	las blusas rojas

Possessive adjectives: These adjectives operate according to the same rules of agreement; however, possessive adjectives are always placed *before* the nouns they modify. Study the following paired sets of English and Spanish examples. Note that a singular and a plural adjective phrase is provided for each possessive adjective; *nuestro*, the only of the possessive adjectives that ends with an *–o*, is the only adjective which will generate four forms.

English Possessive Adjectives			Spanish Possessive Adjectives		
	SINGULAR	PLURAL		SINGULAR	PLURAL
FIRST PERSON	my mother my father my parents	our uncle our aunt our uncles our aunts	FIRST PERSON	mi madre mi padre mis padres	nuestro tío nuestra tía nuestros tíos nuestras tías
SECOND PERSON	your brother		SECOND PERSON	tu hermano	

	your sister your siblings			tu hermana tus hermanos		
THIRD PERSON	his grandfather his grandmother his grandparents her grandmother her grandfather her grandparents	their cousin (m.) their cousin (f.) their cousins (m.) their cousins (f.)		THIRD PERSON	su abuelo su abuela sus abuelos su abuelo su abuela sus abuelos	su primo su prima sus primos sus primas

You'll note that there is some amount of redundancy among the third person singular and plural possessive adjectives – *su* expresses *his, her,* and *their* interchangeably. This does take some getting used to, but always keep in mind that the possessive adjective applies to *the item or person that is owned*, not the person who owns it.

Demonstrative adjectives: As the name suggests, demonstrative adjectives help designate the number of items to which you refer. You'll recall these same words from the previous discussion regarding demonstrative pronouns. Simply remember that adjectives will be used along with nouns whereas the pronouns replaced the nouns and were used alone. First, compare the English and Spanish demonstrative adjective sets.

this / these here – indicating an item that is close to the speaker		
	SINGULAR	PLURAL
MASCULINE	este	estos
FEMININE	esta	estas

that / those there – indicating an item that is at a short distance from the speaker		
	SINGULAR	PLURAL
MASCULINE	ese	esos
FEMININE	esa	esas

that / those over there – indicating an item that is at a significant distance from the speaker		
	SINGULAR	PLURAL
MASCULINE	aquel	aquellos
FEMININE	aquella	aquellas

Now, as you take a look at some examples of the demonstrative adjectives in context, remember that the golden rule of agreement still applies. Also notice that quite a bit of information is implied with the simple use of a demonstrative adjective that would require additional words to accomplish in English.

¿Prefieres _estos_ zapatos aquí o _aquellos_ zapatos allá?

Do you prefer _these_ shoes _here_ or _those_ shoes _over there?_

Me gustan _esos_ zapatos que tiene Mamá.

I like _those_ shoes that Mom has.

¿Cuáles de las galletas quieres? ¿_Esas_ galletas con chocolate o _aquellas_ galletas con canela?

Which of the cookies do you want? _These_ chocolate cookies (_there_) or _those_ cinnamon cookies (_over there_)?

No quiero ningunas de _esas_ galletas. Quiero _estas_ galletas de menta.

I don't want any of _these_ cookies. I want _these_ mint cookies (_that are right here_).

Verbs

If you talk with anyone who has ever spent time in a language classroom, the first aspect they are likely to bemoan is the concept of verb conjugation. It is a concept that is about as foreign to English speakers as, well... Spanish. This is for the sole fact that we do not readily recognize a dramatic pattern of conjugation in our own language. Yet, if you stop to think about it, these changing verbs do exist in the most simple of our infinitive verbs – "to be." You would never consider stating "I be from the United States;" you intuitively conjugate the verb and know that you should say "I am from the United States." An added benefit of this system of unique verb endings is that frequently the subject pronouns are omitted from usage with the verb form. While **yo hablo** conveys "I speak," **hablo** provides the same message.

Firstly, do not fear the jargon that accompanies this section. An *infinitive* is merely an un-conjugated form of a verb. In English, you can identify an infinitive as *any* verb preceded by the word "to" – to speak, to dance, to sing. In Spanish, any infinitive will be a verb which ends -*ar*, -*er*, or -*ir*.

Secondly, understand that *to conjugate* simply means to break apart into usable forms: the infinitive "to be" generates the forms *am, are, is, was, were, will be, etc.*

A *verb tense* simply refers to a timeframe – present (what a person *does*), preterit (what a person *did*), imperfect (what a person *was doing*), future (what a person *will do*), and conditional (what a person *would do*).

In Spanish you will encounter infinitives and verb conjugation, just in a very large, highly formulaic system of unique verb endings. Infinitives are divided into three classes (-*ar*, -*er*, -*ir*) and many tenses that allow us to refer to different timeframes. The overwhelmingly vast majority of verbs in Spanish are regular – that is to say that they will follow the same pattern of conjugation. Once again, it is best to recognize the general and overriding sameness among verb forms rather than fretting about irregularities.

In order to conjugate verbs, you will follow the same two-step process for present, preterit, and imperfect tenses. Again, observe that each of the tenses denotes a different timeframe.
> **STEP 1:** Remove the ending from the infinitive form of the verb (-*ar*, -*er*, -*ir*)
> **STEP 2:** Attach the ending that corresponds to the subject of the verb. Notice that the patterns among the three classes of verbs are similar to each other.

Present tense: Once you know that the present tense of the verb *hablar* indicates that a person "speaks," "is speaking," or "does speak," you now only need to know what the other infinitives mean in order to be able to use them: *bailar* (to dance), *comer* (to eat), *romper* (to break), *vivir* (to live), and *subir* (to climb, to go up).

	-AR VERBS		-ER VERBS		-IR VERBS	
	hablar	bailar	comer	beber	vivir	subir
yo	hablo	bailo	como	bebo	vivo	subo
tú	hablas	bailas	comes	bebes	vives	subes
él, ella, Ud.	habla	baila	come	bebe	vive	sube
nosotros, nosotras	hablamos	bailamos	comemos	bebemos	vivimos	subimos
ellos, ellas, Uds.	hablan	bailan	comen	beben	viven	suben

Preterit tense: The preterit tense is the first of two past tenses. Here, the preterit indicates that a person "spoke" or "did speak."

	-AR VERBS		-ER VERBS		-IR VERBS	
	hablar	bailar	comer	beber	vivir	subir
yo	hablé	bailé	comí	bebí	viví	subí
tú	hablaste	bailaste	comiste	bebiste	viviste	subiste
él, ella, Ud.	habló	bailó	comió	bebió	vivió	subió
nosotros, nosotras	hablamos	bailamos	comimos	bebimos	vivimos	subimos
ellos, ellas, Uds.	hablaron	bailaron	comieron	bebieron	vivieron	subieron

Imperfect tense: The imperfect tense works along with the preterit to explain the past tense. Here, the imperfect indicates that a person "was speaking" or "used to speak."

	-AR VERBS		-ER VERBS		-IR VERBS	
	hablar	bailar	comer	beber	vivir	subir
yo	hablaba	bailaba	comía	bebía	vivía	subía
tú	hablabas	bailabas	comías	bebías	vivías	subías
él, ella, Ud.	hablaba	bailaba	comía	bebía	vivía	subía
nosotros, nosotras	hablábamos	bailábamos	comíamos	bebíamos	vivíamos	subíamos
ellos, ellas, Uds.	hablaban	bailaban	comían	bebían	vivían	subían

The future and conditional tenses follow a slightly different pattern. Instead of dropping the infinitive ending, keep it in its place and then add the new conjugation endings to the end of the *entire* infinitive. Notice that it makes no difference whether you are working with an *–ar*, *-er*, or *–ir* verb, endings for both the future and the conditional remain the same.

Future tense: The future tense simply explains what will happen in the future...that a person "will speak."

	-AR VERBS		-ER VERBS		-IR VERBS	
	hablar	bailar	comer	beber	vivir	subir
yo	hablaré	bailaré	comeré	beberé	viviré	subiré
tú	hablarás	bailarás	comerás	beberás	vivirás	subirás
él, ella, Ud.	hablará	bailará	comerá	beberé	vivirá	subirá
nosotros, nosotras	hablaremos	bailaremos	comeremos	beberemos	viviremos	subiremos
ellos, ellas, Uds.	hablarán	bailarán	comerán	beberán	vivirán	subirán

Conditional tense: The conditional tense explains what could happen, many times with a certain additional requirement placed upon the action, for example, *I could speak if I were sufficiently prepared.*

	-AR VERBS		-ER VERBS		-IR VERBS	
	hablar	bailar	comer	beber	vivir	subir
yo	hablaría	bailaría	comería	bebería	viviría	subiría
tú	hablarías	bailarías	comerías	beberías	vivirías	subirías
él, ella, Ud.	hablaría	bailaría	comería	bebería	viviría	subiría
nosotros, nosotras	hablaríamos	bailaríamos	comeríamos	beberíamos	viviríamos	subiríamos
ellos, ellas, Uds.	hablarían	bailarían	comerían	beberían	vivirían	subirían

Present subjunctive: The formation of the present subjunctive is more complicated than other tenses. In order to create these forms, begin with the first-person singular form of the present tense and drop the –o from the end. Then, proceed to add the new endings that are indicated in the charts below. In general, you'll notice that these are very similar to the present tense endings just reversed: *-ar* verbs take *-er/-ir* endings and *-er* and *-ir* verbs take *-ar* endings.

	-AR VERBS		-ER VERBS		-IR VERBS	
	hablar	bailar	comer	beber	vivir	subir
yo	hable	baile	coma	beba	viva	suba
tú	hables	bailes	comas	bebas	vivas	subas
él, ella, Ud.	hable	baile	coma	beba	viva	suba
nosotros, nosotras	hablemos	bailemos	comamos	bebamos	vivamos	subamos
ellos, ellas, Uds.	hablen	bailen	coman	beban	vivan	suban

A more detailed explanation of the usage of the subjunctive appears later in this guide.

Compound tenses

In addition to the five simple tenses which use only one verb, there are also the compound tenses which are formed with the helping verb **haber**. The most common of these compound tenses are the present perfect and the pluperfect. In order to form these compound tenses, you must conjugate the helping verb into the desired tense and then use the past participle form of the primary verb. Note that the only verb form that actually changes according to the subject pronoun is the helping verb; the past participle remains consistent through all forms.

Present perfect: This compound tense indicates what a person "has done" in the recent past. This action could also have started in the past and is continuing up to the present moment in time. This structure parallels English structure identically:

I have lived in the United States all of my life.	**Yo he vivido en los EE UU toda mi vida.**
I have been to Mexico twice.	**Yo he ido a México dos veces.**
I have never travelled to Ecuador.	**Yo nunca he viajado a Ecuador.**

	-AR VERBS		-ER VERBS		-IR VERBS	
	hablar	bailar	comer	beber	vivir	subir
yo	he hablado	he bailado	he comido	he bebido	he vivido	he subido
tú	has hablado	has bailado	has comido	has bebido	has vivido	has subido
él, ella, Ud.	ha hablado	ha bailado	ha comido	ha bebido	ha vivido	ha subido
nosotros, nosotras	hemos hablado	hemos bailado	hemos comido	hemos bebido	hemos vivido	hemos subido
ellos, ellas, Uds.	han hablado	han bailado	han comido	han bebido	han vivido	han subido

Present perfect subjunctive: This compound tense operates under the guidelines of the subjunctive and indicates "that a person has done." The detailed explanation of the subjunctive appears later in this guide. In order to form these compound verbs, simply conjugate the verb **haber** into the subjunctive.

	-AR VERBS		-ER VERBS		-IR VERBS	
	hablar	bailar	comer	beber	vivir	subir
yo	**he** hablado	**he** bailado	**he** comido	**he** bebido	**he** vivido	**he** subido
tú	**has** hablado	**has** bailado	**has** comido	**has** bebido	**has** vivido	**has** subido
él, ella, Ud.	**ha** hablado	**ha** bailado	**ha** comido	**ha** bebido	**ha** vivido	**ha** subido
nosotros, nosotras	**hemos** hablado	**hemos** bailado	**hemos** comido	**hemos** bebido	**hemos** vivido	**hemos** subido
ellos, ellas, Uds.	**han** hablado	**han** bailado	**han** comido	**han** bebido	**han** vivido	**han** subido

Pluperfect: This compound tense indicates what a person "had done" before another action in the past was completed. Just like the present perfect, this structure parallels English structure as well.

I had known my boyfriend for ten years before we married.

We had lived in an apartment before we purchased our house.

Yo había conocido a mi novio por diez años antes que nos casamos.

Nosotros habíamos vivido en un apartamento antes que compramos nuestra casa.

	-AR VERBS		-ER VERBS		-IR VERBS	
	hablar	bailar	comer	beber	vivir	subir
yo	**haya** hablado	**haya** bailado	**haya** comido	**haya** bebido	**haya** vivido	**haya** subido
tú						
él, ella, Ud.	**hayas** hablado	**hayas** bailado	**hayas** comido	**hayas** bebido	**hayas** vivido	**hayas** subido
nosotros, nosotras						
ellos, ellas, Uds.	**haya** hablado	**haya** bailado	**haya** comido	**haya** bebido	**haya** vivido	**haya** subido
	hayamos hablado	**hayamos** bailado	**hayamos** comido	**hayamos** bebido	**hayamos** vivido	**hayamos** subido
	hayan hablado	**hayan** bailado	**hayan** comido	**hayan** bebido	**hayan** vivido	**hayan** subido

Reflexive verbs

Reflexive verbs are a subset of verbs that once again are very comparable to English. In general, a reflexive verb is any verb whose subject also receives the action of the verb. Frequently, it's easy to envision reflexive verbs if you think of those actions that you must complete in front of the mirror as you take care of personal hygiene – there you are looking at a reflection of yourself in the mirror as you both perform the action (subject) and receive the action (direct object). However, many times the concept of a reflexive verb is applied much more widely in Spanish that it is in English.

Reflexive verbs function in the exact same manner as other verbs, but you will additionally use a reflexive pronoun to accompany the verb. Where the subject pronoun is entirely optional, the reflexive pronoun is required.

Study the following reflexive verbs: **mirarse** (to look at oneself); **lavarse** (to wash oneself); and **vestirse** (to dress onself).

	mirarse	lavarse	vestirse
yo	**me** miro	**me** lavo	**me** visto
tú	te miras	te lavas	te vistes
él, ella, Ud.	se mira	se lava	se viste
nosotros, nosotras	**nos** miramos	**nos** lavamos	**nos** vestimos
ellos, ellas, Uds.	se miran	se lavan	se visten

This concept will apply to all verb tenses – simply conjugate the verb to whichever tense is desired. Note that when you utilize a compound verb, the reflexive pronoun appears *before* the helping verb.

Cuando me cepillo el pelo, me miro en el espejo.

When I brush my hair, I look at myself in the mirror.

Siempre te lavas las manos antes de preparar comida o comerla.

You always wash your hands before preparing or eating food.

Antes que se acostaron, mis hijos se habían vestido en pijamas y cepillado los dientes.

Before they went to bed, my children had dressed themselves in pajamas and brushed their teeth.

Ser v. Estar

One of the particular difficulties of Spanish is managing one of the most basic verbs in English – to be. Spanish splits this concept into two verbs that seemingly mean the same thing, yet upon closer investigation, you'll notice that **ser** and **estar** express completely different concepts. First, study the irregular forms of these verbs in the present, preterit, and imperfect tenses. Note that **estar** is a regular imperfect tense verb and that both verbs are otherwise regular in the future, conditional, and compound tenses.

	IMPERFECT TENSE		PRESENT TENSE		PRETERIT TENSE	
	SER	ESTAR	SER	ESTAR	SER	ESTAR
yo	soy	estoy	fui	estuve	era	estaba
tú	eres	estás	fuiste	estuviste	eras	estabas
él, ella, Ud.	es	está	fue	estuvo	era	estaba
nosotros, -as	somos	estamos	fuimos	estuvimos	éramos	estábamos
ellos, ellas, Uds.	son	están	fueron	estuvieron	eran	estaban

Now, study the differences in usage and understand that each verb performs its own tasks. Generally speaking, **ser** is used in a much broader sense while **estar** handles a much smaller work load, and therefore it is easier to remember its basic usages. The verb **ser** is most commonly used as an identifier and describer of essential traits and characteristics. In addition, it substitutes for the phrase "to take place" when referring to events. Consider the following examples provided in each of the following categories:

- Identifying people, places, and objects

Este es un álbum de fotos de nuestras vacaciones.

This is a photograph album of our vacation.

Ella es mi amiga Mariana.

She is my friend Mariana.

Este es el Museo de Antropología en la Ciudad de México.

This is the Museum of Anthropology in Mexico City.

Esta es La Piedra del Sol.

This is the Sun Stone.

Es el calendario azteca.

It is the Aztec calendar.

- Identifying professions

Mi madre es secretaria y mi padre es ingeniero.

My mother is a secretary and my father is an engineer.

- Identifying possession

No son mis zapatos...¿Son tus zapatos?

They are not my shoes...Are they your shoes?

- Identifying nationality or origin

Originalmente, mis antepasados son de Alemania, pero mi familia es de California. Yo soy de San Diego.

Originally, my ancestors are from Germany, but my family is from California. I am from San Diego.

Mi casa es de ladrillos. Mi escritorio es de madera. Mi ropa es de algodón.

My house is made of bricks. My desk is made of wood. My clothes are made of cotton.

- Identifying day, date, or time

Hoy es lunes. Es el 11 de julio. Son las diez de la noche.

Today is Monday. It is July 11. It is ten o'clock at

night.

- Describing personality traits

  Yo soy una persona muy trabajadora y ambiciosa.

  I am a very hard-working and ambitious person.

- Describing physical appearance

  Yo soy baja, morena y delgada.

  I am short, brunette, and thin.

- Explaining when an event takes place

  La reunión es en la oficina de nuestro jefe.

  The meeting is (takes place) in our boss' office.

In contrast, the verb **estar** explains conditions or states that are not part of the essence – the very being – of what is being described. Consider the following examples provided in each of the following categories:

- Explaining health and other conditions

  Estoy enferma y cansada hoy, pero mañana estaré mejor.

  I am sick and tired today, but tomorrow I will be better.

- Explaining moods and emotions

  Normalmente Marta está de buen humor, pero hoy está muy triste porque su gato está perdido.

  Normally, Marta is in a good mood, but today she is very sad because her cat is lost.

- Explaining locations

El gato está en el árbol que está detrás de la casa.

The cat is in the tree that is behind the house.

- Explaining a condition that results from an action

En este momento, un hombre está llenando el tanque con gasolina mientras otro hombre está limpiando los vidrios.

At this moment, one man is filling the gas tank while another man is cleaning the windows.

- Expressing a verb in the present progressive in order to emphasize an action in progress

Yo tiré una pelota por la ventana y ahora está rota.

I threw a ball through the window and now it is broken.

Se me olvidó el pan en el tostador y ahora está quemado.

I forgot the bread in the toaster and now it is burnt.

Irregular verbs

Even though the overwhelmingly vast majority of verb conjugations are regular, there are a handful of verbs which completely defy the systematic nature of conjugation. Ironically, these troublesome verbs are the most commonly used. The good news is that among these verbs, smaller patterns do arise and this assists in memorizing the differences. In order to best observe the patterns that emerge, it is best to break these verbs down by the different tenses and into their groups of similarity. For simplicity's sake, all verbs presented within this section are defined on this list.

caber	to fit	**oír**	to hear	**ser**	to be
dar	to give	**poder**	to be able; "can"	**tener**	to have
decir	to say	**poner**	to put	**traer**	to bring
estar	to be	**querer**	to want	**valer**	to value
haber	**helping verb	**saber**	to know (a fact)	**venir**	to come
hacer	to do; to make	**salir**	to leave; to exit	**ver**	to see
ir	to go				

Present tense: Be particularly mindful of the irregularities that occur in the present tense because they will impact the conjugation of the present tense subjunctive that will be referenced later.

In this first set of irregularities, the verbs are radically different from the predictable pattern. The commonality among the four verbs is the first-person singular form consistently ending **–oy**.

	ser	estar	ir	dar
yo	soy	estoy	voy	doy
tú	eres	estás	vas	das
él/ella/Ud.	es	está	va	da
nosotros, -as	somos	estamos	vamos	damos
ellos/ellas/Uds.	son	están	van	dan

In the second set, the first-person, singular form shows the common irregularity in becoming *–go*; you'll notice some further problematic spots in the verbs *tener*, *venir,* and *decir* (stem-changing verbs) as well as in the verb *oír*.

	hacer	poner	salir	tener	venir	decir	traer	oír
yo	hago	pongo	salgo	tengo	vengo	digo	traigo	oigo
tú	haces	pones	sales	tienes	vienes	dices	traes	oyes
él/ella/Ud.	hace	pone	sale	tiene	viene	dice	trae	oye
nosotros, -as	hacemos	ponemos	salimos	tenemos	venimos	decimos	traemos	oímos
ellos/ellas/Uds.	hacen	ponen	salen	tienen	vienen	dicen	traen	oyen

In the final set, there is no pattern established and there are no other verbs which share the same endings.

	saber	ver
yo	sé	veo
tú	sabes	ves
él/ella/Ud.	sabe	ve
nosotros, -as	sabemos	vemos
ellos/ellas/Uds.	saben	ven

Present tense subjunctive mood: In this verb set, there are only six truly irregular verbs. However, be careful. As you learned previously, the subjunctive is always based upon the first-person singular form of the present tense indicative. It is because of the high amount of irregularities that occur in that particular form that makes the subjunctive *appear* to be irregular, but you'll notice that so long as the first-person singular form ends with an –*o*, the verbs actually follow the prescribed pattern. The only verbs that are irregular in the present subjunctive are those verbs whose first-person, singular form does not end in an -*o*. However there are many other irregularities that occur to the present tense. Think of the verb *tener* – its first-person, singular form is *tengo*, therefore all of its subjunctive forms will be based upon that verb form. Even though these forms appear odd, because they follow the established pattern, they are not considered to be irregular.

	dar	estar	haber	ir	ser	saber
yo	dé	esté	haya	vaya	sea	sepa
tú	des	estes	hayas	vayas	seas	sepas
él/ella/Ud.	dé	esté	haya	vaya	sea	sepa
nosotros, -as	demos	estemos	hayamos	vayamos	seamos	sepamos
ellos/ellas/Uds.	den	estén	hayan	vaya	sean	sepan

Preterit tense: Beware! This tense is commonly known as the most highly irregular in the language! However, one helpful hint is to notice that absolutely no irregular preterit tense verb carries and accent mark.

In this first set of irregularities, the verbs are radically different from the predictable pattern. The best thing to rely on is that the four verbs are very similar to each other. Indeed, it is strange that both *ser* and *ir* in the preterit tense are identical to each other; discerning between the possible meanings is dependent upon the context in which they are used.

	dar	ir	ser	ver
yo	di	fui	fui	vi
tú	diste	fuiste	fuiste	viste
él/ella/Ud.	dio	fue	fue	vio
nosotros, -as	dimos	fuimos	fuimos	vimos
ellos/ellas/Uds.	dieron	fueron	fueron	vieron

In this second set, the root deviates from the infinitive and becomes *-uv-*.

	andar	estar	tener
yo	anduve	estuve	tuve
tú	anduviste	estuviste	tuviste
él/ella/Ud.	anduvo	estuvo	tuvo
nosotros, -as	anduvimos	estuvimos	tuvimos
ellos/ellas/Uds.	anduvieron	estuvieron	tuvieron

In the third set, the root deviates from the infinitive and becomes either *-us-, -ud-,* or *-up-*.

	poner	poder	saber	caber
yo	puse	pude	supe	cupe
tú	pusiste	pudiste	supiste	cupiste
él/ella/Ud.	puso	pudo	supo	cupo
nosotros, -as	pusimos	pudimos	supimos	cupimos
ellos/ellas/Uds.	pusieron	pudieron	supieron	cupieron

In the fourth group, the *-c-* of the infinitive transforms into a *-j-*; this rule will apply to any verbs that end vowel – *cir*. In the case of *traer*, the *-j-* is added. Additionally, you'll notice that in the third-person, plural form, the ending is simply *–eron* instead of *–ieron*. Verbs which end in a vowel + *–cir* will behave in much the same way (*intruducir, producir, traducir)*.

	decir	traer
yo	dije	traje
tú	dijiste	trajiste
él/ella/Ud.	dijo	trajo
nosotros, -as	dijimos	trajimos
ellos/ellas/Uds.	dijeron	trajeron

Imperfect tense: After having seen the large numbers of irregularities that occur with the preterit tense, the imperfect tense gives you a chance to rest easy...within the whole language there are only three irregular verbs in this tense.

	ir	ser	ver
yo	iba	era	veía
tú	ibas	eras	veías
él/ella/Ud.	iba	era	veía
nosotros, -as	íbamos	éramos	veíamos
ellos/ellas/Uds.	iban	eran	veían

Future and Conditional tenses: For these two tenses, you only need to learn the shared irregular roots; the endings in all cases remain the same as for regular verbs. These are the most commonly irregular verbs for this tense.

In the first group, change the *-e-* of the infinitive to *-d-*.

poner > pondr-   *valer > valdr-*

salir > saldr-   *venir > vendr-*

tener > tendr-

In the second group, eliminate the *-e-* from the infinitive.

caber > cabr-

poder > podr-

saber > sabr-

In the last group, there is no governing rule and each must be learned individually.

decir > dir-

hacer > har-

querer > querr-

Indicative, Subjunctive, Imperative

In addition to dividing a language's verbs into tenses that refer to different timeframes, Spanish further divides its verbs into three different moods which refer to the speaker's attitude toward the action of the sentence. Of the three, the subjunctive is the most difficult for English speakers because we generally do not recognize when it is used in English – it exists, but it is only notably different in a few verbs. The indicative and the imperative are much more readily identified.

Indicative: You use the indicative in much the same way that a reporter creates a news article based on facts and observations which should be verifiable from a number of different witnesses. The indicative may be used in either statements or questions and in any of the aforementioned tenses. Consider the following news lead and notice that every verb relates an event that actually occurred, is occurring, or will occur.

Ayer, el policía detuvo a un ladrón después de recibir una llamada del Banco Nacional. Francisco Rivas confesó que entró al banco con una pistola y demandó todo el dinero. Dijo que necesitaba el dinero para pagar su matrícula a la universidad. Ahora está en la cárcel y mañana se presentará delante del juez del condado.

Yesterday, police detained a thief after receiving a call from the National Bank. Francisco Rivas confessed that he entered the bank with a pistol and demanded all of the money. He said that he needed the money in order to pay his university tuition. Now he is in jail and tomorrow he will present himself before the county judge.

Imperative: You use the imperative to deliver commands and to order behaviors just like an officer in the military...or your mother or teacher, for that matter. Even though we commonly think of people in positions of authority over us to be the only ones to issue commands, nearly every person in the course of a typical day will state a command:

Buenos días, cariño... ¡Levántate!

Good morning, sweetheart...Get up!

Tráigame un café con leche, por favor.

Bring me a coffee with milk, please.

¡Vámonos!

Let's go!

Subjunctive: You use the subjunctive in order to provide an opinion or an emotional reaction to an event or to express that something is contrary to fact. For most English speakers, this concept is entirely baffling because it barely exists anymore in English. Yet, it remains prominently in place in the Spanish language. Comparing the languages is little help because the phrasing is entirely different. The better approach is to learn the Spanish sentence structure with the definite pattern of a formula.

Espero que tú vengas mañana.	*I hope that you come tomorrow.*
Estoy triste que Marcela no pueda asistir a la boda.	*I am sad that Marcela cannot attend the wedding.*
Es bueno que tus padres vengan también.	*It's good that your parents are coming also.*
Recomiendo que Uds. lleguen temprano a la estación de tren.	*I recommend that all of you arrive at the train station early.*
Dudo que haya demora en la salida.	*I doubt that there will be delays in the departure.*
Ojalá que todo les vaya bien.	*I hope that all goes well for you.*

In order for you to use the subjunctive, you must recognize certain characteristics that will always appear in the sentence. First, the sentence is a compound and made up of two clauses – an independent one which initiates the sentence with an indicative verb and a dependent one which contains a subjunctive verb. Each of these verbs must have different subjects and the word *que* connects the two clauses together.

Yo espero	*que tú vengas*	I *hope*	that you *come* tomorrow.
mañana.			
		1	2
1	**2**		

Note that each of the two verbs has separate subjects and appear in separate clauses that are joined together with *que*.

It is important to understand that not all verbs have the capacity to trigger the subjunctive, but some verbs placed a sentence that follows the formula will always trigger the subjunctive. These are easily learned according to the acronym *WEIRDO*. Learn a few of these verbs at first and then you will discover more that fit into these categories – they will function in the same manner.

Wishes	esperar, desear, querer	to wish (hope, expect), to desire, to want
Emotions	estar alegre, estar triste, estar enojado alegrarse, entristecerse, enojarse	to be happy, to be sad, to be angry to become happy, to sadden, to anger
Impersonal expressions	es bueno, es malo, es posible, es imposible, es importante, es interesante, es triste, es urgente	it's good, it's bad, it's possible, it's impossible, it's important, it's interesting, it's sad, it's urgent
Recommendations	recomendar, aconsejar, mandar	to recommend, to advise, to order
Doubts and denial	dudar, negar	to doubt, to refuse
Ojalá	This is an idiomatic word which is used as a verb yet is not a verb. It always will trigger the subjunctive.	Figuratively, **ojalá** means something along the lines of "I wish..." Historically, it comes from a time when the Moorish people who were Muslim inhabited Spain from 711 to 1492. At that time, it meant "O to Allah." Today, it holds no religious significance and is used as a common phrase.

Infinitives, Gerunds, and Participles

Infinitives, gerunds, and participles are verb forms that are used along with other helping verbs in order to express ideas. Each of these special forms will convey the primary idea of the verb without showing either person because they have no subject or tense (because these verb forms remain constant). It is the job of the helping verb to carry the conjugation which shows both person and tense. Each of these verb forms is formed differently and is used in different circumstances.

Infinitives: The infinitive is a key starting place when discussing conjugation. As you learned before, there are three classifications of infinitives: *-ar, -er,* and *-ir.* In addition to being not only the vocabulary you learn and the starting place for all conjugation, it may be used in a verb phrase – these verbs are known as modal verbs. The key rule to remember is that if you use two verbs in direct sequence with each other, always conjugate the first verb (the helping verb) and leave the second verb in its infinitive form. Examine a few examples:

*Este fin de semana, nosotros **vamos a viajar** a Seattle.*	*This weekend, we **are going to travel** to Seattle.*
*Hoy, **tengo que terminar** el trabajo.*	*Today, I **have to finish** the job.*
***Queremos cenar** en un restaurante cerca de la playa.*	*We **want to dine** at a restaurant near the beach.*
*Cuando estamos de viaje, **debemos llevar** nuestro dinero en un lugar seguro.*	*When we are travelling, we **should carry** our money in a safe place.*
*¿**Puedes comprender** bien las direcciones?*	***Can you understand** the directions well?*

Gerunds: You will recognize that a gerund corresponds to verbs in English which end *–ing*. In Spanish, you will form gerunds by dropping the infinitive termination and adding *–ando* to an *–ar* verb and *–iendo* to an *–er* or an *–ir* verb. Commonly, you will use gerunds as part of the progressive tenses (present, past, and future) in order to indicate that an action is, was, or will in progress at the moment indicated. These progressive forms provide an additional sense of immediacy to the verb that the simple tense does not convey.

***Ahora mismo, estoy comiendo** el desayuno.*	*Right now, I <u>am eating</u> breakfast.*
*¡**Me interrumpiste! Estaba hablando** por teléfono.*	*You interrupted me! I <u>was talking</u> on the telephone!*
***En dos horas estaremos asisitiendo** a la*	*In two hours we <u>will be attending</u> the movie.*

película.

Participles: These you will find are the **–ed** equivalents of verb forms that are not the primary verbs in sentences. Like gerunds, they are accompanied by helping verbs. You will usually discover participles in two different structures – the perfect tenses which were explained earlier and the passive voice which will be explained subsequently. In order to form the participles, once again drop the infinitive termination and

add **–ado** to an **–ar** verb and **–ido** to an **–er** or an **–ir** verb. Notice that the first three sentences demonstrate the present perfect tense while the last three show the passive voice.

Yo he vivido aquí por veinte años.	*I have lived here for twenty years.*
He hablado español por treinta años.	*I have spoken Spanish for thirty years.*
Nunca he comido ostras.	*I never have eaten oysters.*
El libro fue publicado en muchos idiomas.	*The book was published in many languages.*
Las galletas fueron comidos por los niños.	*The cookies were eaten by the children.*
España fue invadido por los moros en el año 711.	*Spain was invaded by the Moors in 711.*

Passive Voice

The passive voice is a structure that de-emphasizes the person responsible for the action of a sentence. Because of this, you should tend to use the active voice, which explicitly states the subject of the verb as the person responsible for the action. However, there are cases in which the passive voice is accepted and there are two ways in which to accomplish this sentence structure.

- By using the verb *ser* and the past participle together you will indicate what was done. Notice that in most cases it is unimportant who completed the action; what is important is that the action occurred. It is necessary to notice that because of this structure, the participle now acts as an adjective and must therefore maintain agreement with the noun it modifies.

El edificio <u>fue destruído</u> durante el terremoto.

The building <u>was destroyed</u> during the earthquake.

Don Quijote <u>fue escrito</u> por Miguel de Cervantes.

Don Quijote <u>was written</u> was written by Miguel de Cervantes.

Las familias <u>fueron invitadas</u> a la boda.

The families <u>were invited</u> to the wedding.

- You may also convey general behaviors or expected behaviors through what is known as the passive *se*. This time, notice how the verb form is consistently in the third person, but will vary between singular and plural according to the subject, which invariably will appear *after* the verb this time. Carefully compare the Spanish and English examples. You'll notice that the actual passive voice remains in the English sentences where the Spanish opts for the passive *se*.

<u>Se prohíbe</u> fumar en lugares públicos en los EEUU.

Smoking <u>is prohibited</u> in public places in the United States.

<u>Se habla</u> español aquí.

Spanish <u>is spoken</u> here.

No <u>se aceptan</u> tarjetas de crédito. Solo se acepta dinero en efectivo.

Credit cards <u>are not accepted</u>. Only cash <u>is accepted</u>.

French fries <u>are eaten</u> with

Se comen *las papas fritas con*   *gravy in Canada.*
salsa de carne en Canadá.

Adverbs

The usage of adverbs is based on your knowledge of adjectives – if you know the adjective, you can most likely create the adverb even though you may never have seen or heard it previously. In English, the suffix *–ly* commonly denotes an adverb; in Spanish, you will find that *–mente* works in much the same way. Consider the following examples:

rápido *(quick)*	**rápidamente** *(quickly)*	**cuidadoso** *(careful)*	**cuidadosamente** *(carefully)*
lento *(slow)*	**lentamente** *(slowly)*	**tranquilo** *(calm)*	**tranquilamente** *(calmly)*
orgulloso *(proud)*	**orgullosamente** *(proudly)*	**solo** *(alone)*	**solamente** *(only)*
desesperado *(desperate)*	**desesperadamente** *(desperately)*	**ruidoso** *(loud)*	**ruidosamente** *(loudly)*

You'll easily see that a pattern emerges: in order to transform an adjective into an adverb, drop the final *–o* of the adjective, change it to *–a*, and then add *–mente*. As usual, there are some small exceptions – those adjectives that end in a consonant: *fácil (easy)* becomes *fácilmente (easily).*

In addition to this basic rule, you'll want to memorize the following adverbs that are irregular: *bien (well), mal (badly, poorly), también (also), nunca (never),* and *siempre (always).* As a general rule, place adverbs after the verb; if you utilize two adverbs in the same sentence, place one before and one after the verb.

Mi madre cocina <u>bien</u>. Yo <u>siempre</u> cocino <u>mal</u>.	*My mother cooks <u>well</u>. I <u>always</u> cook <u>poorly</u>.*

The adverbs *sí (yes)* and *no (no)* frequently are overlooked because they are both used intuitively. However, special note must be made about *no.* As much as English speakers are taught to never use double negatives, it is necessary to do so in Spanish. When this is the case, always make sure that *at least one* of the negatives appears before the verb.

Yo <u>no</u> cocino <u>nunca</u>. Yo <u>nunca</u> cocino.	*I never cook.*

No, no es mi chaqueta.	*No, it is not my jacket.*
No veo a nadie.	*I do not see anyone.*

If you consider the literal translations of a few of these sentences, you'll recognize that English would never allow such a sentence structure: **Yo no cocino nunca** literally states *I don't cook never* and **No veo a nadie** is *I don't see no one.* Suffice it to say that no languages ever work in exactly the same fashion and it is wise to simply follow the generalized rules and avoid thinking about it too much.

As you are narrating events and telling a story, it is helpful to use adverbs to establish *when* the action takes place. Here are a few time expressions that will assist you:

ya	*already*	**desde**	*since*
hace tres días (meses, años)	*three days (months, years) ago*	**dos veces al día (mes, año)**	*two times a day (month, year)*

As you saw with other adverbs, the placement of these adverbs is generally immediately before the verb. However, when an adverbial phrase becomes too bulky for the middle of a sentence, it is preferred to place the phrase either at the beginning or the end of the sentence. In some cases, your choice of placement makes no difference and then it is a matter of personal preference; in other cases, choose the location that is most logical to the meaning of the sentence.

Hace cinco años yo fui de viaje en México. Yo fui de viaje en México hace cinco años.	*Five years ago I travelled to Mexico. I travelled to Mexico five years ago.*
Los dentistas recomiendan que nos cepillemos los dientes tres veces al día.	*Dentists recommend that we brush our teeth three times a day.*

Prepositions

Prepositions – words that indicate a time or spatial relationship – by and large are a matter of learning vocabulary. While there are a large number of prepositions, begin by studying the following basic list of paired prepositions.

cerca de (close to)	*delante de* (in front of)	*de* (from)	*sobre* (over)
lejos de (far from)	*detrás de* (behind)	*a* (to)	
			en (in, at, on)
encima de (on top of)	*antes de* (before)	*con* (with)	
debajo de (beneath)	*después de* (after)	*sin* (without)	*contra* (against)
a la derecha de (to the right of)	*al lado de* (beside)		*según* (according to)
	enfrente de (across from)		
a la izquierda de (to the left of)			

Grammatically speaking, what you must pay attention to now is that a preposition will be followed by a noun, which will likely be accompanied by an article. When this is the case, you'll need to be on the lookout for the potential to make a contraction between the prepositions "de" and "a" with the masculine, singular definite article. Observing examples is the best way to learn this subtle detail of grammar.

Mi casa está cerca __del__ lago. Está lejos __de la__ montaña.	*My house is close to the lake. It is far from the mountain.*
Mañana voy __a la__ playa; no voy __al__ cine.	*Tomorrow I'm going to the beach; I'm not going to the movies.*

Even though the usage of most prepositions is fairly transparent, the usage of **por** and **para** remains quite elusive to even the most seasoned Spanish-speakers. The two prepositions seem to be virtually interchangeable – many simply believe that both mean "for" – and yet, just like the verbs *ser* and *estar* they divide the burden of work between themselves. Understanding the concept behind each is more helpful than enumerating the list of possible translations. So, with that in mind, figure that **por** typically indicates motion through an area and refers to the route or means; on the other hand, **para** usually indicates a destination, a purpose, or a time limit. Now consider the following examples for each of the prepositions:

POR

- route (through, along, by)

Vamos a andar <u>por</u> el parque pero Ana y Julio van a andar <u>por</u> el río. Cuando vamos de compras, podemos pasar <u>por </u>tu tienda favorita.	*We are going to walk <u>through</u> the park but Ana and Julio are going to walk <u>along</u> the river. When we go shopping, we can stop <u>by</u> your favorite store.*

- means of transportation or transmittal (by)

Preferimos viajar <u>por</u> avión.	*We prefer to travel <u>by</u> plane.*
Te voy a mandar la información <u>por</u> correo electrónico.	*I am going to send you the information <u>by</u> e-mail.*

- Point of temporary stop (through)

Cuando volamos a Buenos Aires, tenemos que pasar <u>por</u> La ciudad de México.	*When we fly to Buenos Aires, we have to go <u>through</u> Mexico City.*
Mientras hago las compras, tengo que pasar <u>por</u> el banco y los correos.	*While I do the shopping, I have to stop <u>by</u> the bank and the post office.*

- Duration of time (for)

Vivíamos en Guatemala <u>por</u> seis años.	*We lived in Guatemala <u>for</u> six years.*

Vamos de viaje <u>por</u> dos semanas.	*We are traveling <u>for</u> two weeks.*

- Rate (per)

Se puede manejar a 75 millas <u>por</u> hora en una autopista.	*You can drive 75 miles <u>per</u> hour on a freeway.*
Los precios <u>por</u> galón de gasolina son altísimos.	*The prices <u>per</u> gallon of gasoline are really high.*

- Equal exchange or trade (for)

Compré los pantalones <u>por</u> cuarenta dólares.	*I bought the pants <u>for</u> forty dollars.*
Te daré mi chicle <u>por</u> tus caramelos.	*I'll give you my gum <u>for</u> your candy.*

- Substitution ("on behalf of" or "in place of")

Voto <u>por</u> el mejor candidato.	*I'm voting <u>for</u> the best candidate.*
Roberto trabaja <u>por</u> Elena porque ella está enferma.	*Roberto is working <u>for</u> Elena because she is sick.*

PARA

- Destination (to, for)

Los astronautas viajaban para la luna.	*The astronauts traveled <u>to</u> the moon.*
Mañana salimos para Nueva York.	*Tomorrow we leave <u>for</u> New York.*

- Purpose (in order to)

Yo necesitaba estudiar mucho para sacar buenas notas.	*I needed to study <u>in order to</u> get good grades.*
Siempre trabajamos mucho para tener éxito.	*We always work hard <u>in order to</u> be successful.*

- Time limit (by, for, on, before)

¿<u>Para</u> cuándo necesitas el artículo?	*When do you need the article <u>by</u>?*
Lo necesito para la reunión que tengo el jueves.	*I need it <u>for</u> the meeting that I have on Thursday.*
¿Puedo traértelo para el miércoles?	*May I bring it to you <u>on</u> Wednesday?*
Sí, lo necesito para las tres.	*Yes, I need it <u>by</u> three o'clock.*

- Personal opinion (for)

<u>Para</u> mí, creo que tener hijos es un gran placer.	*<u>For</u> me, I think that having children is a great pleasure.*
<u>Para</u> nosotros, es mejor que no vayamos juntos.	*<u>For</u> us, it's best that we not go together.*

Conjunctions

Conjunctions serve to connect and glue words, phrases, or clauses together. For the most basic understanding, concentrate on learning *coordinating conjunctions,* which will help you join words and phrases together in lists and will assist you in combining simple sentence structures together. Begin with learning the vocabulary:

o...o	either...or	*y*	and
ni...ni	neither...nor	*también*	also
pero	but		

When using most of these conjunctions, it will be fairly intuitive and come naturally to you. Observe a few examples before examining the rules that accompany them.

¿Quieres comer helado o galletas?	*Do you want to eat ice cream or cookies?*
No quiero comer ni helado ni galletas. ¡Yo quiero comer helado y galletas!	*I don't want to eat ice cream or cookies. I want to eat ice cream and cookies!*
No voy a ir a la heladería pero voy a la panadería.	*I am not going to the ice cream shop but I am going to the bakery.*
	Well, I am going to the ice cream shop and the bakery also!
¡Pues, yo voy a ir a la heladería y a la panadería también!	

As you work with these conjunctions, there are a few rules to keep in mind:

- *Either...or (o...o)* does not have to appear in pairs, however the conjunction may. The following is a possible variation: *¿Quieres comer o helado o galletas?* Usually you will provide the second *o* in order to add emphasis.
- *Neither...nor (ni...ni)* should always appear in pairs.
- There are variants of *o* depending upon the initial letter of the word that follows it. Whenever the next word begins with an *o-* or the equivalent sound generated by *ho-*, the conjunction is changed to *u* in

order to ease pronunciation: ***¿Neceistas siete u ocho dólares?****(Do you need seven or eight dollars?)* Additionally, if you are using this conjunction with numerals, the conjunction is changed to ***ó*** in order to alleviate any confusion with the numeral 0: ***¿1970 ó 1971? ¿En qué año naciste?*** *(1970 or 1971? In which year were you born?)*

- Likewise, whenever ***y*** is followed by a word that begins with the letter ***i-*** or the equivalent sound generated by ***hi-***, the conjunction is changed to ***e*** in order to ease pronunciation. ***¿Vienen Marcos e Inés? Sí, y mis hijos e hijas también.*** *(Are Marcos and Inés coming? Yes, and my sons and daughters too.)*

Cardinal and Ordinal Numbers

Counting in Spanish is a matter of simply learning the cardinal numbers. As you do so, you'll see that here, too, a pattern emerges. Once you learn the basics, you'll be able to count nearly endlessly. First, start by learning the words for the numbers from zero to twenty:

zero	**cero**		
one	**uno**	eleven	**once**
two	**dos**	twelve	**doce**
three	**tres**	thirteen	**trece**
four	**cuatro**	fourteen	**catorce**
five	**cinco**	fifteen	**quince**
six	**seis**	sixteen	**dieciséis**
seven	**siete**	seventeen	**diecisiete**
eight	**ocho**	eighteen	**dieciocho**
nine	**nueve**	nineteen	**diecinueve**
ten	**diez**	twenty	**veinte**

It's helpful to note that for the numbers sixteen through nineteen, the words are actually comprised of a simple math sum: dieciséis literally is "ten and six"...16. Apply this thought as you continue to count to thirty and beyond:

twenty-one	**veintiuno**	thirty-one	**treinta y uno**	forty-one	**cuarenta y uno**
twenty-two	**veintidós**	thirty-two	**treinta y dos**	forty-two	**cuarenta y dos**
twenty-three	**veintitrés**	thirty-three	**treinta y tres**	forty-three	**cuarenta y tres**
twenty-four	**veinte y cuatro**	thirty-four	**treinta y cuatro**	forty-four	**cuarenta y cuatro**
twenty-five	**veinte y cinco**	thirty-five	**treinta y cinco**	forty-five	**cuarenta y cinco**

This same pattern continues as you count the rest of the way through twenty-nine, thirty-nine, and forty-nine, including all of the way up to ninety-nine. So, all that remains is to learn the numbers that represent each of the multiples of ten: *cincuenta* (50), *sesenta* (60), *setenta* (70), *ochenta* (80), *noventa* (90). Additionally, apply the following other multiples and subsequent rules:

- *Cien* (100) refers to precisely the number 100; when the number exceeds 100, utilize *ciento:*
  146   *ciento cuarenta y seis*   198 *ciento noventa y ocho*
- Logically, you will find the hundreds to be fairly predictable, however note that 500, 700, and 900 vary slightly in formation: *dos cientos* (200), *tres cientos* (300), *cuatro cientos* (400), *quinientos* (500), *seis cientos* (600), *setecientos* (700), *ocho cientos* (800), *novecientos* (900).
- Beyond the hundreds, you will encounter *mil* (1.000), *millón* (100.000), and *billón* (1.000.000).
- Finally, notice that the separation that is normally represented by a comma in English is represented by a period in Spanish. Likewise, the decimal point is unexpectedly a comma: 1,92 = 1.92.

Ordinal numbers are used in order to indicate the order in which items fall within a list. Generally speaking, this too is a matter of learning vocabulary, but be careful as these are usually used as adjectives and therefore must maintain agreement with the nouns which they modify.

first	**primer**	sixth	**sexto**
second	**segundo**	seventh	**séptimo**
third	**tercer**	eighth	**octavo**

fourth	**cuarto**	ninth	**noveno**
fifth	**quinto**	tenth	**décimo**

Follow these additional rules:

- The masculine singular forms of *first* and *third* are always **primer** and **tercer**; only when they are nouns are the forms **el primero** and **el tercero** allowed.
- Just as we use the numerical abbreviations in English (1st, 2nd, 3rd, etc.), there are numerical abbreviations in Spanish. However, note that when these abbreviations are adjectives, even the abbreviation shows agreement with the antecedent: *1er lugar, 2a avenida, 4o piso*.

In addition to learning the cardinal and ordinal numbers, there are also other vocabulary words that help to indicate quantities. Because these are adjectives, be sure to maintain agreement.

mucho (many)	**Hay muchas personas que hablan español.** *There are many people that speak Spanish.*
poco (few)	
	Hay poca gente en la iglesia hoy. *There are few people in church today.*
otro (another)	
	Necesito otro lápiz, por favor. *I need another pencil, please.*
ningún (no; none)	
	Ningún hombre me abrió la puerta. *Not one man opened the door for me.*
algún (some)	**Algunos jóvenes jugaban en el parque.** *Some youngsters were playing in the park.*

Syntax

Syntax simply refers to the appropriate word order that must be used in order for a sentence to make sense. While you will find that many of these rules are similar to English, some of these defy what you instinctively know.

- Declarative sentences simply make a statement. At the core of the sentence, you will begin with a subject and a verb and follow with any direct and indirect objects, adding in prepositional phrases or adverbs as desired. Remember, the biggest obstacle is to place any adjectives *after* the nouns they modify. Observe how each element is added into this basic sentence.

Mi padre compró una bicicleta.	*My father bought a bicycle.*	subject-verb-direct object
Mi padre compró una bicicleta roja.	*My father bought a red bicycle.*	adjective added
Mi padre compró una bicicleta roja para mí.	*My father bought a red bicycle for me.*	indirect object added
Ayer mi padre la compró para mí.	*Yesterday, my father bought it for me.*	adverb added; direct object pronoun substitution included
Ayer mi padre me la compró de la tienda Rojas.	*Yesterday my father bought it for me from the Rojas store.*	indirect object pronoun substitution and prepositional phrase included

- Interrogative sentences ask questions. There are several ways in which to phrase a question.
  - Voice inflection may be used in any question which only requires an answer of yes or no. As a statement, a speaker's voice remains at a constant pitch. Without re-ordering the words of a sentence a speaker is able to imply that he is asking a questions simply by raising his or her voice at the end of the question:

Eres alumno en de la universidad.	*You are a student at the university.*
¿Eres alumno de la	*Are you a student at the university?*

universidad?   My keys are on the table.

                                       My keys are on the table?

Mis llaves están en la mesa.

¿Mis llaves están en la mesa?

- o Inversion must be utilized when using interrogative pronouns: *¿dónde? (where?), ¿cuándo?*
  (when?), ¿por qué? (why?) Inversion occurs when the order of the subject and verb are
  reversed:

¿Dónde están mis llaves?   Where are my keys?

¿Cuándo es la película?   When is the movie?

¿Por qué no vamos nosotros un   Why don't we go a little bit later?
poco más tarde?

- o If the interrogative pronoun is *¿qué? (what)* or *¿quién(es)? (who)*, inversion is not required
  because the words *¿qué?* and *¿quién?* function as the subject of the sentence.

¿Qué es la capital de Argentina?   What is the capital of Argentina?

¿Quién es el presidente de la   Who is the president of the company?
compañía?

- Exclamatory sentences show excitement. There is no variation in common syntax; however, exclamatory
  sentences frequently begin with the word *qué*. Rather than expressing *what?* as an interrogative
  pronoun, it expresses *how* as an exclamation.

¡Qué raro!   How strange!

¡Qué interesante!   How interesting!

¡Qué rico!   *How delicious!*

Conclusion

With this basic grammar, we hope we have given you enough information to get you started on your Spanish-learning journey, or have refreshed your memory. Now get out there and start talking!

About Minute Help Press

Minute Help Press is building a library of books for people with only minutes to spare. Follow @minutehelp on Twitter to receive the latest information about free and paid publications from Minute Help Press, or visit minutehelpguides.com.